Valley Forge, Gettysburg
place names resonate w... ... .
And now the Twin Towers of the World Trade Center,
another battleground of the fallen and of the heroic.

Remembering Abraham Lincoln's words at
Gettysburg in 1863:

> "...*that we here highly resolve that these dead*
> *shall not have died in vain—that this nation,*
> *under God, shall have a new birth of freedom—*
> *and that government of the people, by the people,*
> *for the people, shall not perish from the earth.*"

We pay tribute to our heroes, the living and the dead,
past and present.

This journal provides a place for you to reflect, and to
record your notes, your thoughts, ideas, inspirations
and dreams.

**The Viesti Collection, Inc. pledges twenty-five percent
of all receipts from this journal, or all profits, whichever
is greater, to The Twin Towers Fund. In the aftermath of
the events of September 11, 2001, The City of New York has
established The Twin Towers Fund to accept contributions
for the victims and families of the firefighters, police
officers and emergency medical technicians who are the
first heroes in the present conflict.**

George Washington Statue, Washington Cathedral, Washington, D.C.

Statue of Liberty, World Trade Center, New York, New York

Campfire, Revolutionary War Reenactment, Valley Forge, Pennsylvania

Sentry, Revolutionary War Reenactment, Valley Forge, Pennsylvania

Washington Crossing the Delaware Reenactment, Trenton, New Jersey

Reenactment of the Battle of Trenton, New Jersey

Revolutionary War Reenactment, Fort Ticonderoga, New York

Revolutionary War Reenactment, Fort Ticonderoga, New York

Revolutionary War Reenactment, Fall River, Massachusetts

Boston Tea Party Ship, Boston, Massachusetts

The Alamo, San Antonio, Texas

Fort McHenry National Monument and Historic Shrine
(birthplace of U.S. National Anthem, 1812), Baltimore, Maryland

Cannon silhouette, Gettysburg National Memorial Park, Gettysburg, Pennsylvania

Monument, Gettysburg National Memorial Park, Gettysburg, Pennsylvania

Fort Pulaski National Monument, near Savannah, Georgia

Lincoln Memorial, Washington, D.C.

64

USS Arizona Memorial, Pearl Harbor, Honolulu, Hawaii

Cemetery at Omaha Beach, Normandy, France

Memorial to The 1st Infantry Division, Washington, D.C.

The Iwo Jima Memorial, Arlington, Virginia

M47 tank, General George Patton Museum, Chiraco Summit, California

Medal of Honor Museum, Chattanooga, Tennessee

The Korean War Memorial, Washington, D.C.

The Vietnam War Memorial, Washington, D.C.

Soldier, Veterans Day, Arlington National Cemetery, Arlington, Virginia

Iranian Hostages Ticker Tape Parade, New York, New York

Gulf War Ticker Tape Parade, New York, New York

Twin Towers, World Trade Center, New York, New York